WHAT YOUR AGENT
WILL NOT
TELL YOU ABOUT
COLLEGE
ADMISSIONS

Joe M. Klunder and Rachel A. Winston, Ph.D.

LIZARD PUBLISHING

Written by: Joe M. Klunder and Dr. Rachel A. Winston
Designed by: Michelle Tahan

Lizard Publishing is not sponsored by any college or outside organization. While all data was derived by school, state, national, and internationally published sources, some statistics may be out of date, since published sources vary widely as to the date of submission and currency of student demographics. Every attempt was made to obtain the best information during the writing of this book from the Institute for International Education's OpenDoors, U.S. Office of Homeland Security, U.S. Department of Education, UK Council of International Student Affairs, China Scholarship Council, Common Data Set, College Board, Wall Street Journal, Foreign Policy, Newsweek, Journal of College Admissions, college/organizational sites, and college representatives. Descriptions and anecdotes are a compilation of student, faculty, and staff interviews and may vary from other individual impressions as each perspective is unique. Even so, we have sought to triangulate as many points of light as possible. If you would like to share your insights into student experiences, colleges, or facts to be included in the next edition of this book, we invite you to write us at the address below or at the e-mail address: info@mylizard.org.

ISBN 978-1-946432-01-8

Lizard Publishing®
7700 Irvine Center Drive, Suite 800
Irvine, CA 92618
www.lizard-publishing.com
Printed in the U.S.A.

Lizard Publishing is a premium quality provider of educational reference materials, student written work, and motivational publications for global learners, parents, counselors, educators, and stakeholders in education.

Our mental process is fueled by three tenets.

1. Ignite the hunger to learn and the passion to make a difference
2. Illuminate the expanse of knowledge by sharing cutting edge thinking
3. Innovate to create a world that may only exist in our dreams

Lizard Publishing creates, designs, produces, and distributes books and resources to provide academic, admissions, and career information. We work with educational leaders who transform the educational landscape to publish relevant content and advise students of their educational and professional options, with the aim of developing 21st century learners and leaders. We also work with students to publish their books and present widely diverse ideas to the college/graduate school bound community.

With headquarters in Irvine, California, Lizard Publishing works virtually with authors to edit, publish, and distribute both digital and hard copy books and other print and electronic resources.

Acknowledgements

We thank everyone for their generous time in looking over this work and contributing with ideas and suggestions. By working with passionate educators, we have learned and improved this work. Each individual below added to the vibrancy, authenticity, and perspective.

Frederika Cazemier, University College, Groningen
Rebecca D. Hansen, Northern Kentucky University
Jason Holly, Hong Kong International School
Jayne Klunder, Saddleback College
Ethan Lei, Former Liaison at Beijing Public High School 80
Marjorie Smith, Denver University
Jonathan Sy, Universitas College Counseling, Philippines
Michelle C. Tahan, Lizard Publishing
Kristoffer Toribio, Orange Coast College

Preface

This book is dissimilar, or even directly against, many of the rumors, hearsay, and testimonials that claim the college admissions process is completely fair. While most individuals who work in admissions are noble and genuinely committed to a just and ethical process, even within the ranks of admissions officers there exist pockets of questionable admissions practices and enrollment management priorities that may seem unfair when viewed from the outside. Students and parents, clamoring to gain admission at all costs and by any means, combined with agents who are paid by universities to bring students to their school and also by parents, have generated deep concern about unprincipled behavior in the college admissions process. This environment has promoted fraud and unethical behavior among "professionals" across all dimensions of the college admissions arena.

In 2016, Reuters and other major news agencies reported cheating on tests and instances of agents paying off admissions representatives for preferential admissions. This revelation has exposed widespread corruption, particularly in China. Organizations like the College Board and ACT have disqualified tests in China on a massive scale. These instances have caused hundreds of students to lose their chance for admission or at least to have to retake the test at a later date. Students who are already attending college, but have been found to have cheated on admissions tests or any part of the admissions process face the possibility of being disciplined or expelled.

Advertising by agents and unethical "advisors" is often misleading. They convince thousands to pay $50,000+ for "guaranteed" admissions to college. At the same time, these agents are paid by universities to bring students to their school. Some lure in parents and take their money for the dream of college admission. The contract a parent signs is one price, but ends up being much more expensive than originally stated. Additionally, these agents often make claims they cannot keep. Some, though certainly not all, "advisors" in the Chinese for-profit education system act in ways that are illegal, unethical, and looked down upon in the West. In fact, many in admissions want to have nothing to do with agents.

In the pages that follow, we shine a light on the work of agents and what students and parents need to know before signing a contract. Contained in this quick and readable book is valuable information for students, parents, counselors, advisors, and university staff members to consider in order to understand the landscape of international college admissions. We also present information for those parents hiring agents to make better decisions about who to hire and the danger of being pulled into an unethical scheme.

This book is designed to provide viewpoints about Western education that are common knowledge among many professionals in the field, yet are sometimes either accidentally or purposefully ignored by agents and their employees. There is no intention to claim that all agents are bad; some are very good, honest, and truly care about their clientele. However, with the rash of scandals, test score cancellations, and expulsions of students from U.S. colleges due to cheating, we decided to write this book to provide readers with more information. We also plan to expand this book later to include additional data collected from our research.

We hope that by reading this book, students and parents can make more informed choices. The contents will provide insights into agents, ethics, and relationships between various constituents. Thus, this book is meant to be a cautionary and introductory discussion into the ethics of paying huge fees for "college placement," or worse, breaking a rule that may result in the student being expelled for a violation of a university's code of academic integrity.

The tone of this work may seem provocative. Yet, we designed these contents to encourage critical thinking, open discussion, and further investigation of a very complex and often ill-defined process. These skills also happen to be the hallmarks of traditional Western liberal education.

If you have any questions, please contact either one of the authors:

Joe Klunder at joe.m.klunder@gmail.com
or
Dr. Rachel A. Winston at drwinston@mylizard.org

About the Authors

Dr. Rachel A. Winston is a professor, researcher, and statistical analyst who writes and publishes books and articles on various aspects of education. As a scientist, mathematician, and leadership expert, she has been a professor of college counseling, mathematics, and engineering as well as a trusted global college admissions consultant. She trained counselors around the world teaching in the UCLA College Counseling Certificate Program.

With more than three decades of experience in higher education, she has taught at major universities in the United States. As a mathematician, she won the Cryptanalyst Award at a National Science Foundation program in Bletchley Park, England.

Living in Europe and the Washington, D.C. area and traveling to a hundred countries throughout her life, her broad range of experience has made her one of the leading cross cultural consultants. Starting college at thirteen and winning the National High School Senior of the Year from the American Legion, she has studied at more than a dozen colleges including: Harvard, UCLA, USC, NYU, GWU, and Syracuse as well as graduate school in China. Dr. Winston holds a Ph.D. from the University of Texas at Austin and has numerous master's degrees, including her 2016 M.S. in Publishing from The George Washington University.

In her Southern California community, she served on the Board of Directors of the Newport Beach Chamber of Commerce, Leadership Tomorrow, and the Faculty Association of California Community Colleges, and was also the Education Committee Director with the Costa Mesa Chamber of Commerce. She served the Regional Coordinator for the Mathematical Association of America. Prior to coming to California she worked on Capitol Hill, the White House, and the U.S. Department of Labor. She won the 2012 McFarland Literary Achievement Award and has spoken at over a hundred local and national meetings and conferences. Dr. Winston published her first mathematics book in the 80s and spends her life serving and inspiring students to achieve their college and career goals.

About the Authors

Joe M. Klunder has lived and taught in six countries: South Korea, Saudi Arabia, Turkey, Libya, United States, and China. This work is designed as a reflection of his commitment to understanding more about the world. Joe believes that education is an avenue that allows people to come together from across the world and voice opinions in a systematic forum.

Receiving his B.A. in History from Brown University, Joe has had over six years of experience teaching over 500 students English, history, and psychology, as well as mentoring dozens of students as they pursue international study. He has spent his last three years in China working at both public and private schools as a teacher and college admissions counselor.

He has started five community service projects, which involve creating social change through free basic health care, education services, and networking referrals. He created and maintains a free website, basicedhelp. org, to assist in providing services and referrals for basic education in English, Spanish, French, Arabic, and Chinese. He also maintains three personal websites:joeklunder.com, joeklunder.net, and joeklunder. org. The first site includes information about his professional and educational career, the second about his reflections from traveling around the world, and the third about his international philanthropy.

Joe has met remarkable people wherever he has gone. The most inspiring individual he has encountered has been his former student and friend from South Korea, Carl Ahn, who has traveled to over 100 countries and lived for extended periods in several foreign countries. Carl is an example of how Joe believes all people should pursue living life to the fullest by being genuinely enthusiastic, living a healthy lifestyle, and being generous and supportive to others.

Joe works for Lizard Education College Counseling Center as the International Program Liaison, coordinating speaking engagements in China and consulting students on admissions in China. He is especially keen on forming partnerships with both renowned and lesser known educational organizations around the world.

Contents

Chapter 1

A Brief Introduction to
the Landscape of Agents
and International College
Admissions

A Brief Introduction to the Landscape of Agents and International College Admissions

You might have heard that special introductions, permissions, connections, or foundation donations can get students into a good college. You might have met an agent who promised to help with an easy and "guaranteed" way to gain acceptance. Maybe someone you know was admitted to Harvard, Stanford, Yale, Princeton, Cambridge, Oxford, or another prestigious school by working with an agent who claimed they had "special connections" with admissions and promised that they possessed unique tactics nobody else had. Or, maybe an agent said that, with a payment of a sum of money, your child would be a certain admit.

A 2011 report in *The Journal of College Admissions* entitled, *"College Application with or without Assistance of an Educational Agent: Experience of International Chinese Undergraduates in the US,"* states that 60 percent of Chinese students who attended postsecondary institutions in the United States used an agent in the process of coming to school. The mass hiring of agents has been prompted by the fear that, without help, students would not be accepted to college and future job prospects would be limited. There is increasing concern that Chinese students will be shut out of colleges and the only way to get to the United States, United Kingdom, or other international destination is to pay an agent tens of thousands of dollars to have that chance.

Agents have changed the landscape of college admissions, created big businesses, and made a ton of money by advertising claims that they have huge successes at the top schools around the world with back-door connections. The looming question is whether the student's best interests are served in the process. While many agents do succeed in getting students into college, these acceptances are rarely at the very top schools. There are thousands of colleges with high acceptance rates. Thus, students have a high probability of acceptance with or without an agent.

Advisors, though, can help provide additional information and clarify what is offered at colleges. These advisors are often skilled and knowledgeable about how to access admissions resources, like application procedures, submission deadlines, and testing strategies, as well as find specific programs that suit a student's interests, including summer programs, academic research, internships, and science contests. Some even offer valuable career, interest, and personality testing. Therefore, the most important objective is to find a school where the student will have the best experience, fit into the academic community, learn valuable skills, and be prepared for his or her desired career.

Advisors can provide important information. However, it is important to distinguish between those who put the students' best interest first and those who take advantage of students and their parents. Thus, the problem does not stem from advisors who support students in their investigation and understanding of the process, it is: (1) with agents who take money from the student and also from the college to gain admission, sometimes when the college is not even a good fit for the student and (2) when there is corruption, cheating, and other unethical behaviors behind the scenes.

The following list provides a few reasons why you should be careful.

Ten Reasons Why You Should Beware!

1. **Promises, Promises** – Many agents make promises, but do not deliver on what you expect. Be clear about what you assume to be the outcome and read the fine print in the contract.

2. **High Fees ≠ Acceptances to Top Schools** – Agents charge fees and offer a guarantee that often does not equal acceptances into "good fit" schools. There is a belief among some individuals that, the higher the price, the better the service. This is not always true.

3. **Contracts You Cannot Break** – Fees for services are often much higher than presented in an initial meeting or on a website. The biggest problem is, once you sign up, you are bound to their program. Thus, if they add extra services, you are compelled to pay more. Many times you cannot back out of the contract, even if the services are unfulfilled.

4. **Connections and Back Doors** – Some colleges pay agents to deliver students. A recent Reuters' news series highlights how some companies have committed fraud by buying access to admissions officers. If you do not believe this is a problem, then you do not realize how serious people in the West

consider this behavior. If discovered, the student can be kicked out of college. However, to prevent overgeneralization, this topic will be discussed in more depth later in the book.

5. **Unethical Agent Application Practices** – Cheating, lying, copying, and plagiarizing on the application are just a few unethical practices in which some agents engage.

6. **Widespread GAC/ACT Cheating** – The widespread cheating on tests has become a growing problem and admissions officers are very concerned. For example, in Fall 2016, the Global Assessment Certificate and ACT test, which can cost $10,000 for registration, test preparation, flights, and hotel stays in the testing city, was found to have widespread cheating. Some scores were cancelled and students were not accepted by U.S. colleges or forced to sit for the test at a later date.

7. **SAT Test Scores Cancelled** – In 2015, SAT tests were cancelled and some existing scores were subsequently nullified from 45 test centers in China and Macau. A similar incident happened with the ACT in the fall of 2016 when the tests were disqualified.

8. **Not Trustworthy** – Chinese families say that reputation of the agent or advisor is the most important factor in choosing whom to hire. You want to ask yourself, "Do I trust this person? Do other people who have worked with the agent trust him or her after the admissions process?" When you ask for references from past students, are you only given the names of a couple students who were accepted at a top school? Find out from others and ask questions. Students and parents communicate with one another and have a close network. Ask their friends.

9. **Deceptive Practices** – Test prep centers are often hard to distinguish from agents since many of these have joined together. They solicit students to get in the door to prepare for tests and then encourage the student to hire them for college admissions advising and "guaranteed" admission. These centers may promise a high score, which is done by giving incoming students a hard practice test to prove that he or she needs help, followed by an easy practice test after their test prep to prove that the company did a good job.

10. **Fabricating Entire Applications** – Accepting ghostwritten essays, plagiarizing someone else's writing, making up activities and involvements that never happened, and exaggerating on the application in order to appear qualified,

are just a few examples. United States colleges take this seriously and, if found out, these students are often dismissed from their college.

The number of Chinese students choosing to study abroad for high school and college has increased significantly, although there are some signs that this increase will slow down. According to the Chinese Ministry of Education, 523,700 Chinese students chose to attend higher education institutions outside of China in 2015. Of these, approximately 8 percent were funded by the government or employers and the rest at the family's expense. Approximately three-fourths of these students return to China after school. These students are affectionately called "sea turtles".

The process of applying to Chinese universities is very different than applying for entrance into U.S., U.K., Canadian and other Western schools. The Chinese college entrance exam, GaoKao, a four-day test, typically given in June, is offered to Chinese high school students at the end of their schooling. Tackling a dozen subjects, these students intensely prepare for and take a single test that determines their college-going future. Top scorers earn a seat at China's prestigious universities. Decades ago, few students came to the United States for college. Those students were typically graduate scholars in a specific field. Now, going to the United States and the United Kingdom for college has become more common and competitive.

There are many reasons, but primarily, this stemmed from the 2008 financial crisis. Due to the funding model of American postsecondary institutions, budgets were tightened. Decreasing public monies changed the landscape of education, particularly at state colleges and universities. Colleges and universities needed to find new resources to fill their programs with students who were willing to pay the full cost of education. International students fit the criteria. This led to recruitment bonuses for bringing in students and the expansion of the educational agency model.

According to the Institute for International Education, in the 2015-2016 school year, 1,043,839 international students attended U.S. colleges with 31.5 percent from China. The international student population attending U.S. post-secondary institutions represents 5.2 percent of the total higher education population. Similarly, the UK Council of International Student Affairs reports that the number of international students studying in the United Kingdom totals 436,585, which is 19 percent of the college student population. Each year, for the past ten years, the number of students coming to the United States from China has steadily increased. Data from the U.K. also

Guaranteed Admission Is Considered Unethical

Guaranteed admission to college is considered unethical. When an individual is paid off in the process of gaining admission, that admission can be nullified. This is also true for paying someone to write a paper/essay or take a test.

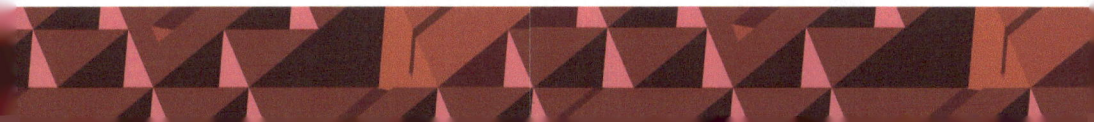

shows a comparable steady increase in Chinese students with 20.5 percent coming from China in the 2014-2015 school year.

Data from the U.S. Department of Homeland Security and published in *Foreign Policy* show the following rankings of college enrollment by numbers of visas for the 2014 - 2015 school year.

Ranked Order of Number of Chinese Student Enrollment by Ivy League School

1. Columbia University – New York, NY
2. Cornell University – Ithaca, NY
3. University of Pennsylvania – Philadelphia, PA
4. Harvard University – Cambridge, MA
5. Yale University – New Haven, CT
6. Brown University – Providence, RI
7. Princeton University – Princeton, NJ
8. Dartmouth College – Hanover, NH

Ranked Order of Number of Chinese Student Enrollment by U.S. Colleges and Universities

1. University of Illinois Urbana-Champaign (UIUC) – Champaign, IL
2. University of Southern California – Los Angeles, CA
3. Purdue University – West Lafayette, IN
4. Northeastern University – Boston, MA
5. Columbia University – New York, NY
6. Michigan State University – East Lansing, MI
7. Ohio State University – Columbus, OH
8. University of California, Los Angeles – Los Angeles, CA
9. University of Indiana Bloomington – Bloomington, IN
10. University of California, Berkeley – Berkeley, CA

11. New York University – New York, NY

12. Pennsylvania State University – State College, PA

13. University of Minnesota, Twin Cities – Minneapolis, MN

14. University of Washington, Seattle – Seattle, WA

15. Arizona State University – Tempe, AZ

16. University of Michigan, Ann Arbor – Ann Arbor, MI

17. Boston University – Boston, MA

18. Illinois Institute of Technology – Chicago, IL

19. Rutgers State University – New Brunswick, NJ

20. University of Texas, Dallas – Richardson, TX

21. University of Wisconsin, Madison – Madison, WI

22. University of California, San Diego – La Jolla, CA

23. Carnegie Mellon University – Pittsburgh, PA

24. State University of New York – Stonybrook, NY

25. Syracuse University – Syracuse, NY

The reality is that Chinese high school and post-secondary students provide financial resources that significantly impact college towns, providing important resources to colleges and the surrounding regions. According to the U.S. Department of Commerce, in 2015, international students added more than $30 billion to the United States economy.

Tackling the Concern By Admissions Officers

Admissions officers presenting at National Association for College Admission Counseling (NACAC) conferences have expressed serious concern regarding the actions of agents and strongly suggested that colleges abandon the practice. However, with so many colleges using agents, a special commission was appointed. They recommended that, rather than disallowing the use of incentive-based compensation for international student recruiting, the ban should be lifted, yet they also cite that the practice should not be encouraged.

Twenty Most Popular Destinations for International Students at U.S. Colleges and Universities in 2014 - 2015 and 2015 - 2016

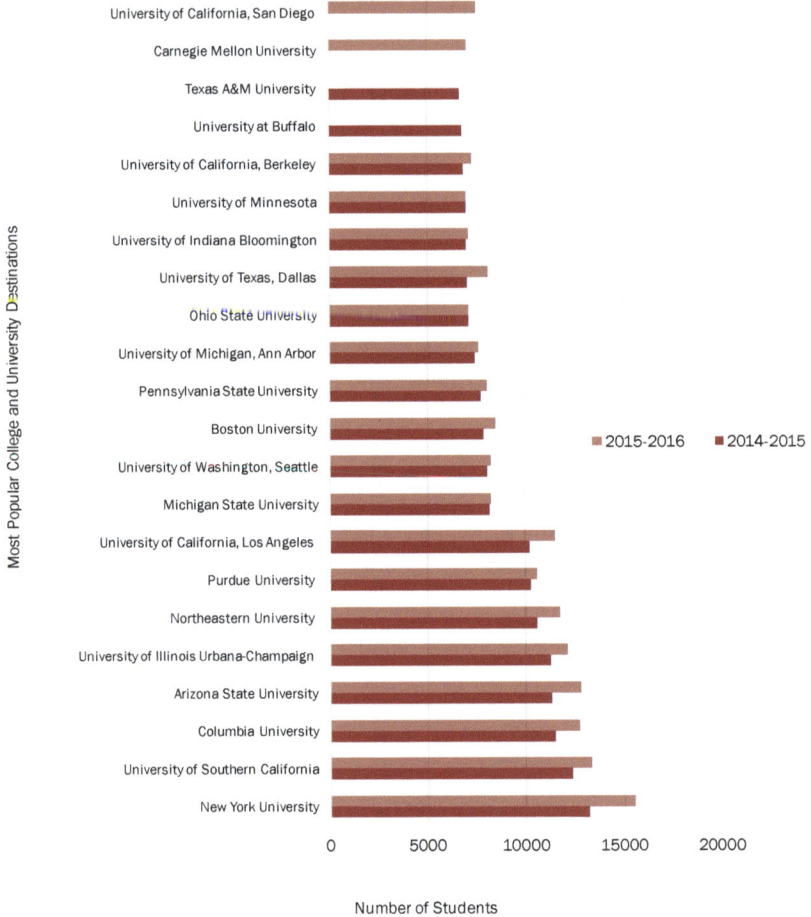

University of California, San Diego
Carnegie Mellon University
Texas A&M University
University at Buffalo
University of California, Berkeley
University of Minnesota
University of Indiana Bloomington
University of Texas, Dallas
Ohio State University
University of Michigan, Ann Arbor
Pennsylvania State University
Boston University
University of Washington, Seattle
Michigan State University
University of California, Los Angeles
Purdue University
Northeastern University
University of Illinois Urbana-Champaign
Arizona State University
Columbia University
University of Southern California
New York University

Most Popular College and University Destinations

■ 2015-2016   ■ 2014-2015

0   5000   10000   15000   20000

Number of Students

Source: Institute for International Education, Open Doors Report

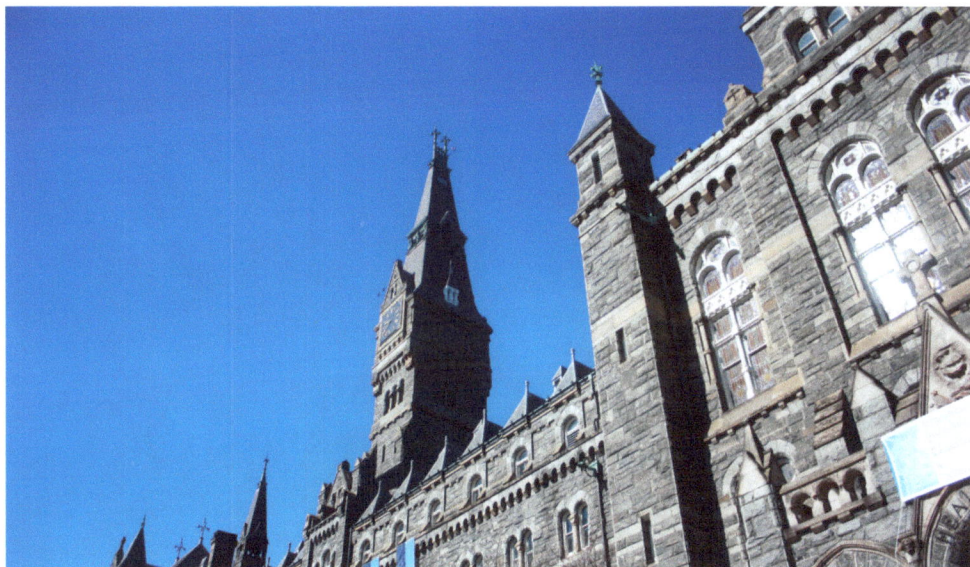

Photo Credit: Michelle C. Tahan

Organizations like the American International Recruitment Council (AIRC) certify agencies around the world and safeguard students and parents by promoting ethical standards. This organization has about 270 institutional members and 80 certified agencies in more than 90 countries. Additionally, professional conferences around the world promote ethical practices, like **WEBA** (World Educate Business Association), and bring together agents, institutions, and study abroad counselors to meet and share their programs.

The Beijing Overseas Study Service Association (BOSSA) created professional standards and a process to verify the documents submitted by Chinese students. They also created a training course, known as the China Education Agent Course (CEAC). To date, approximately 220 agents are now officially certified. China's study abroad industry is growing and the demand for certified agents is also increasing. The CEAC, launched in January 2015, granted its first 100 certificates to agents in the first year after completing its courses and exam. CEAC is recognized by BOSSA, ICEF, and the Chinese Ministry of Human Resources.

The acknowledgment by NACAC and certifications for agents is a step forward, though the professionalism of educational consulting continues to be called into question.

Chapter 2

There is No Best
University in the World;
Look for a Good Fit

There is No Best University in the World; Look for a Good Fit

Fit is a term used by many universities and college counselors to mean a college or university where a student will succeed academically, fully involve themselves in the collegiate environment, and enjoy the experience of classes, majors, and students at that school. Fit is different for each student and has nothing to do with the *U.S. News and World Report* rankings. Only by researching school options can a student know whether or not they are a fit. Visiting campuses helps immensely, but is not always possible.

Twenty Types of College Research

College research may include (not an exhaustive list):

1. Scanning college websites
2. Watching virtual tours
3. Hearing/reading student testimonials
4. Asking questions to college officials
5. Talking to admissions representatives at college fairs
6. Checking the admissions profile for demographics and academic requirements (College Scorecard, College Navigator, Big Future)
7. Soliciting feedback from current students, parents, and alumni
8. Visiting the campus
9. Viewbook, guidebook, or other publication
10. Facebook, Instagram, or other social media
11. Sports coach
12. High school teacher or counselor

13. Faculty member/researcher at the college

14. Magazine or news stories

15. Interview - online or on campus

16. College event, hotel reception, or open house

17. Leadership, sports, academic camp or summer classes

18. Religious event or clergy member

19. Cappex or Zinch

20. College Week Live

There are literally thousands of post-secondary institutions in the world – more than 7,250 in the United States alone, according to the U.S. Department of Education's National Center for Educational Statistics. Colleges and universities vary widely. Researching schools is imperative.

Here are some things to consider:

Location	Support services	Religion
Climate	Sports	Political awareness
Size	Social life	Diversity
Cost	School spirit	Freshman retention
Faculty	Safety	Graduation rate
Majors	Social/Environmental Justice	Difficulty of classes
Classes	Competitiveness	Ease of flying in/out of school
Academic programs	Class size	Dormitory life
Activities	Friendliness	Housing and meal plans
Facilities and resources	Proximity to activities	Major metropolitan center
Student life	Types of students	Fun

Rankings and Ratings

What makes a school famous? For example, most people have heard of Oxford, Cambridge, Harvard, Stanford, Princeton, Yale, Berkeley, and UCLA. Engineers, space experts, and computer scientists have heard of the California Institute of Technology (Cal Tech) or Massachusetts Institute of Technology (MIT).

However, few have heard of Bard College at Simon's Rock, which is an intellectually rigorous liberal arts college, Colorado College and Cornell College, where the 3 1/2 weeks-per-course academic schedule allows students to concentrate on one class at

Considering College Selection Variables

Any competent, experienced and ethical university admissions officer, college counselor, or family member will emphasize that choosing a good undergraduate education goes far beyond rankings, alumni networks, and location.

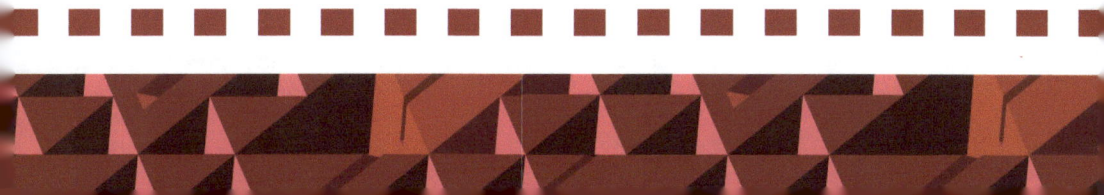

a time, or Sweet Briar College, a women's liberal arts college on a large plantation known for its horseback riding program and seven riding teams. There are literally hundreds of not well known, but very special schools with beautiful campuses that offer an excellent education.

Yet, rankings are based upon a set of quantitative criteria that eliminate much of the subjectivity of the college experience. This elaborate computation of class rank, test scores, reputation, retention, graduation rate, student-faculty ratio, and other variables does not accurately determine either (a) student success (b) fit, (c) satisfaction, (d) career outcome, or (e) student engagement.

Photo Credit: Michelle C. Tahan

A college education is an opportunity to learn and discover what a student enjoys doing, issues that are important to them, and what they want to pursue throughout their life. However, at the same time, a prestigious college education is still perceived by many as the most important ticket to success. Frankly, the world is changing as are credentials, required training, and skill set development to prepare for a transformational work environment. At one time there might have been a single ticket to success and it might have been enrollment at a prestigious university. However, if there ever was ever a

Not Too Secret Fact

For some colleges fundraising, donations, and building endowment funds are institutional priorities that are rewarded. At these schools, though not so flattering, the donations received are considered in the admissions process.

single ticket to success, it was cashed in long ago. At this moment in time, the key to obtaining a well-paying job and fulfilling career after graduation is a function of many factors. Here are ten key requirements: (1) initiative, (2) discipline, (3) persistence, (4) writing, (5) critical thinking/analysis, (6) quantitative reasoning, (7) teamwork, (8) personality, (9) innovation, and (10) technical skills.

There are many factors that determine whether or not a college is a good fit. Ask questions, do research, and seek advice from qualified college counselors who have a broad perspective of admissions.

Photo Credit: Michelle C. Tahan

Often family, friends, and acquaintances offer advice after only attending or visiting a couple of colleges. In other cases, advice is based purely on personal concerns, like proximity, costs, and friends. Some genuinely have your best interest at heart, but base recommendations solely on the rankings provided online, not knowing the reasoning, methodology, or fit. Those who offer this advice often make suggestions out of goodwill, though their perspective is not wide. Thus, it is valuable to talk to someone with a broad range of experience like admissions professionals or certified college counselors, many who have conducted significant research, visited colleges, attended conferences, gathered data from other professionals, and accessed college

Fact About Admissions Officers

Most admissions officers are highly principled. It is very important to these college officials that they remain ethical and balance their often conflicting goals.

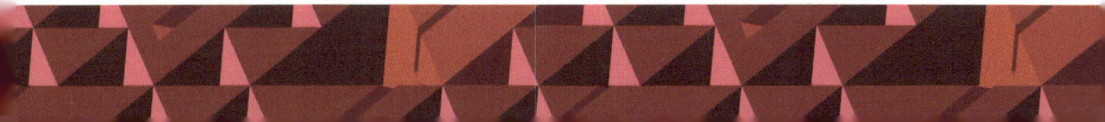

counseling industry information.

Both of the authors of this book have counseling experience, graduate training in the college counseling field, and have an education from Ivy League institutions. We can attest that there are far more important factors in career and life than attending a prestigious school. The prestige of a school may be a source of pride, but not a ticket to certain wealth or happiness.

Finding a passion and pursuing it with vigor is probably the clearest pathway to personal fulfillment. Having supportive people around you is another. Neither has anything to do with attending a college or university that was established a few centuries ago.

Endowments and Donations

Many colleges have endowments that supply the needed resources to maintain their ability to attract and retain faculty, upgrade their facilities, offer scholarships to top students, and build new programs. Donations are important to colleges and those in the foundation office know which families are likely to make a contribution and who will ultimately support the college financially with donations well into the future. Without this, colleges cannot secure their legacy and, in the meantime, host the grand activities that make them enticing to students. Alumni fundraising remains in the background of a college's successful expansion, technology upgrades, ability to attract top faculty, and services offered to students. College officials are grateful to those who donate to their foundation or institutional advancement offices, though there are unwritten rules (and some are actual laws) to which "gratefulness" may be shown.

A few Oxford graduates privately explained that Oxford University officials were discussing how to become more like United States universities. Specifically, some individuals on different levels of administration at Oxford want a more centralized organization with more widespread fundraising efforts in order to increase their endowment, stabilize funding, and attract top quality faculty.

Oxford clearly has an advantage in that they have a worldwide reputation as one of the top five universities. The specific rank of Oxford varies depending upon the source and criteria. While Oxford may also want to increase its size and enrollment, there are disadvantages. Larger schools have clear benefits like broader opportunities and larger constituency of alumni, but they also create bureaucracy and inefficiencies. Smaller schools offer more personalized service, but lack the diversity of courses and programs.

Many Ivy League colleagues complain that competition for donations and funding creates unfair advantages. Sometimes donors, influential alumni, or admissions officers push college standards. This puts colleges in an uncomfortable position because they need money. The complexity of this dilemma is possibly where some agents may attempt to influence schools to look away regarding admissions, academics, requirements, or even problems students create on the campus. The debate about enforcing subjective and often varied perspectives on "traditional educational values" continues.

Colleges and universities strive to maintain their value-centered approach to education. Yet, they must raise money to build their endowments. They must seek grants, external funding, and donations. Most attempt to do this in the most ethically responsible way, despite recent news reports of corruption, fraud, and unethical behavior.

Photo Credit: Michelle C. Tahan

Chapter 3

The Goal of Educational Counseling

The Goal of Educational Counseling

Agents often offer college counseling services. The breadth and depth of this varies widely. There is a difference, though, between agents and traditional college counselors. The main difference is that independent college counselors do not take money from colleges in exchange for encouraging students to attend their school.

The professional field of college counseling is designed to provide a service that helps students learn about opportunities they may not have considered and create a plan to prepare for and be accepted to college. You should find out whether or not the "college counselor" is incentivized by colleges to have you choose and attend their school.

In selecting a college counselor, you should find one who is in tune with your needs and has the breadth of knowledge to help you reach your goals. Educational professionals should be able to help you prepare for your vision of success.

Some agents truly are trained admissions professionals and college counselors. Some have even completed extensive certification programs and their reputation is backed by an organization. However, there are many without credentials. Thus, agents cannot be clumped into one category, in the same way as you cannot stereotype all Americans, Hispanics, Asians, or any other group. Yet, it is common practice for people to villainize this whole group. The intent of this book is not to typecast, but to have you become conscious of the differences and motivations of those you hire. However, most people in the admissions field believe that the work of agents is a dirty game and they want nothing to do with commission-based acceptances.

Besides, there are many reasons why a college may want to work with agents. Some of those are not dishonest or immoral. Colleges need to recruit students. Often, international recruitment plans include sending representatives around the world to meet with students in person. With boots-on-the-ground, the college has a representative who can personally get a feel for students in that area. However, it is not practical for them to fly to every city in every country. Some colleges are particularly interested in attracting students from a particular region and, because of dialect or cultural familiarity, it is simply better if a local person who knew the area could step in and help. Also, sometimes a college is not well known in other parts of the world and they need a person who can communicate the value of their school directly to local counselors, parents, and students. Lastly, advertising and promoting a college requires knowledge of the nuances of that region's tastes and attitudes.

For this reason, colleges often look to agents to do this type of tailored connectedness and send them leads. Since it costs money to travel to schools, the agent is compensated, which is not unreasonable. However, there is a major difference between paying for agent's expenses and convincing students to attend a school because of the payoff they will receive.

Here is a list of universities that are members of a council that works with agents:
http://www.airc-education.org/institutional-members

It is easy for Oxford University, for example, to say that they would never use an agent, since they have a worldwide, outstanding reputation. Yet, not everyone can get accepted to Oxford and most colleges around the world are not well known to parents and students. Unfamiliar does not mean bad. It may just mean that they are small and spend more money on providing a great education than promoting themselves. In fact, most strive to be excellent learning environments. One way to check if the basic, legal educational requirements in a given country are met is to look for the highest accreditation. If it is not accredited, then the university has not met the basic standards from year to year.

The Fine Line of Ethics in College Counseling

There is a significant difference between an agent and a professional college counselor. The fact that agents double dip in taking money from parents and colleges causes many admissions officers, high school counselors, and independent college counseling professionals to be on edge. This line of ethics in college counseling unnerves those who cast the first stone without looking deeper into the individual counselor or their experience.

Agents are typically paid a commission for each student they bring to the colleges that hire them. Their job is different than a certified college counselor who must sign a

Stereotyping Agents

Not all agents are the same. Some are highly professional and ethically minded. Distinguishing competent professionals from unscrupulous salespeople is necessary.

"statement of ethics" saying that they will not take money from a college to "recruit" a student.

Agents are rewarded for the number of students they recruit rather than solely paid for the advice they offer. Thus, agents take money from the school AND take money from families. This double-dipping irks college counseling professionals and university admission officers even more.

The difference is subtle, but important. The agent's role is to help a *college* build their enrollment first and foremost. They may help students too, as they are paid by families, but their additional bonus pay comes from colleges. Before any family makes the decision to choose an agent, certified college counselor, or tutoring center advisor, learn more about what they know, what they offer, and if they are paid to bring in students to a specific school.

The eventual goal for any student is to find and attend a college where they fit in well, meet interesting students, get involved in projects, and gain thought provoking and/ or useful insight from professors. Preparing for graduate school is another significant goal for many students wanting to pursue medicine, dentistry, law, MBA, research, or other graduate programs.

Photo Credit: Michelle C. Tahan

Ultimately, success in college requires hard work, discipline, organization, authenticity, and commitment. True and lasting progress takes years of effort and sacrifice, not months or weeks of special tricks and paying people off. A certified college counselor with many years of experience in the admissions process can be a benefit to families seeking college and university options. However, there are also many free resources available from various nonprofit organizations, government sources, college websites, and school counseling offices. Taking advantage of these saves time and money.

Professional College Counseling

Trained and experienced college counselors have a wide scope of knowledge that includes college choices and admissions requirements. However, many times they are also well versed in opportunities regarding specific majors, careers, internships, scholarships, sports, research, activities, and chances to continue on to medical school, law school, MBA programs, and M.S./Ph.D. options.

In the professional field of college counseling, advisors do not do the work for the student, though they may teach techniques on how to improve essay writing skills and show you how to put your thoughts together to create unique, authentically inspired essays.

Professional college counselors are governed by a personal code of ethics, backed by organizations like IECA, HECA, and NACAC, which provide guidelines of professional conduct for the profession. Check to see if the counselor you hire is a member of one of these three professional organizations or similar organizations overseas. Furthermore, the top college counselors are most often recommended and referred by students and parents who have hired them in the past because of their expertise, wisdom, and value they offer clients.

Reputation

It is a counselor's reputation that attracts others, not flashy ads and promises. Every day, college counselors must do a good job or they do not keep their clients. Reputations are quickly spread through the ranks of families. Those who are excellent and experienced are typically fully booked in the fall, since applications are due and there is a rush to perfect applications and essays from September through December.

New and less experienced independent counselors may have openings because they are just beginning a practice. Some may have outside experiences, but it is important to find out more about their background before you decide. Of course, starting earlier in the year or even a few years ahead of time is preferable so that preparation and planning can be more effective and cover more of the student's long-term goals. Students and families should know about college options and plan a schedule for testing, summer programs, interviews, college visits, essays, and other aspects of the admissions process.

Note that bad reputations are spread throughout student, parent, and counseling communities as well. Bad reputations can be uncovered through research. Professional college counselors should not make promises that are not quite true with results that are not quite what you were told to expect. Some college advisors or coaches are unsuccessful at helping students gain admission to school. They are not as talented as they profess, lie about their credentials, and are known to be incompetent or deliberately deceitful. Sometimes you will not know, but without asking, you will not find out.

When a counselor is very good, people know. However, both agents and professional college counselors must market their services. Word-of-mouth is the most frequent and effective type of marketing. Some, though, are discovered through the media, advertising, books, articles, workshops, and educational meetings. Note also that some advisors of various types make promises they cannot keep like claiming that they can "guarantee" admissions to Ivy League universities, offer services that they cannot fulfill, and provide 24/7 availability.

Goodwill and Good Advice

Goodwill is intangible, but many times you know it when you see it. Though hard to quantify, goodwill is an asset that strengthens a relationship and builds trust. A good counselor can even remain life-long friends with a student after the admissions process is over. You want to know that the college counselor you choose will provide advice that is honest, even when it is not what you want to hear. Parents want to know that their child is brilliant and sometimes they are. However, people exhibit a spectrum of talents and abilities: intellectual, social, academic, athletic, creative, and innovative. Few people are at the top of each of these areas. You can capitalize on your strengths when you choose a college and major that will support your interests and skill set.

Free Resources

There are many types of free resources available from nonprofit organizations, government sources, college websites, and school/university counseling offices.

For example, some students would not be a good fit for a rigorous college that includes active class discussion and hundreds of pages of reading each night. The right college counselor for you is one who provides you this information and also both serves and understands your interests, strengths, and weaknesses. Four years of college is a significant commitment in time, money, academic pursuit, social adaptation, and travel. There are hundreds of excellent college choices that may be far better than an Ivy League school in terms of quality of life throughout the college experience and both career potential and life outcomes after college.

This business relationship should be based on goodwill and good faith on both sides. You should seriously consider whether or not to sign a contract if the agent or college counselor is indebted to a college, coerces you to attend a particular school, forces you to pay upfront, refuses to refund your money, and does not provide the services they advertise. Even if the refund is only for the unused hours, the counselor is demonstrating, to some extent, that they are intent on serving your needs rather than just taking your money. Contract clarity is paramount. However, counselors do have an expectation that they will be compensated for hours they have already worked.

Skill Building to Prepare for College

Experienced, professional college counselors have been through the college admissions process many times. They can help you to learn how to be more organized throughout your college search and application process. They will help you determine the right questions to ask so that you can take the initiative and be more competent.

They may give you a calendar of tasks and deadlines, but you are to learn from that systemized process so that you can make organized calendars in college to keep your own schedule and complete all of your projects. You can learn a great deal from an experienced college counselor in terms of how to accomplish tasks, conduct credible research, remain focused, develop skills, gain discipline, and be successful. With so many admissions, scholarship, financial aid, and summer/gap program deadlines, counselors need to have information at their fingertips. Their independent college advising business depends upon this type of efficiency and he or she is there to help you reach your goals.

Everyone Wants a Guarantee

People want a guarantee for their phone, car, friends, family, and college admissions. However, at least in human interactions, it really does not work that way. Guaranteed college admission is considered unethical.

Ultimately, it is you, the student who must go to college and be prepared to adjust to a new world where the bell does not ring and nobody keeps track of your progress but yourself. You must learn valuable academic, social, and organizational skills that college advisors can teach. Your parent is not going to college with you. Even if parents pay for the services and eventually for your college education, the focus should be on finding the best match for you.

Communication is another important skill to have throughout this process. Breakdowns happen and problems arise when there is too little communication and understanding throughout the application process. The parent can and should provide insights and input. Additionally, the counselor should communicate with the parent so that everyone is on the same page and there are no misunderstandings. Otherwise, there could be tension, distrust, and frustration.

The Promise of Ivy League Admissions

The pressure to get into a good college starts early in China. The strict and disciplinary "tiger mom" and "wolf dad" parenting provides the added push that has put the primary, child raising focus on choosing the most effective and successful educational pathway to a good career starting with kindergarten. This effort starts before a child even begins school. Rather than accepting the free, strict, traditional Chinese education with mountains of homework and extreme pressure, some parents have chosen alternative private educational avenues. Now in high demand, these alternative schools are increasing in popularity.

China's rapid and impressive development has changed the socioeconomic status of families. Many students want to go West for college. With increasing access to money to pay for college, families have more choices for higher education. The entire globe of colleges and universities await with a plethora of options. Many countries offer enticing options with career changing possibilities, worldly perspective, and fluency in other languages. Particularly in countries where English is used throughout the college education, the possibilities are limitless. Families in China are discovering that this English language skill can open important and impressive doors to greater success and business opportunities.

However, there are differences in culture and perspectives in the areas of business, education, ethics, and communications. The way many Chinese families have come to navigate their own political and social systems is different from the method of operations and administration in the West. As greater understanding, relationship building, and alliances are constructed between Asia and the West, there will be greater clarity in communications.

Regarding admissions into Western higher education programs, the process is very different than the one for Chinese students entering colleges in China. Most colleges in the United States and Great Britain require an application, essay, testing, and information to determine student interests, involvements, and motivations. These colleges appreciate authenticity, passion, intellectualism, and character. To enter college in China, on the other hand, requires taking one test, the Gaokao.

Every student can attend college if they choose to do so. There are openings each year, even after almost all of the applications are submitted. However, the goal of a professional college counselor is to find a college where the client will thrive and find success.

There are tens of thousands of colleges in the world. One of these is right for you.

Unprofessional and Unethical Consulting

First, it is unethical to promise results. In the end, it is an admissions committee, almost never a single admissions officer and certainly not an agent that will decide if a student's application is accepted. Many agents do not live by these guidelines. They should not make promises they cannot keep just to get you to sign up with them.

Second, counselors and agents should not falsely encourage students to apply to colleges in which there is almost no chance of admission. While it may seem hypocritical for top-ranked colleges to write letters and call students to convince them to apply, knowing that they have no chance of being accepted, or athletic coaches encouraging students to apply Early Decision when the chances of attending or playing sports there are negligible, they see this as blanket recruitment efforts intended to ensure that there are enough applicants.

Without adequate qualifications, there is virtually no chance. Some students do not have the credentials to be accepted. Success is questionable too, particularly when classes are graded on a curve. Your advisor should be upfront with you about a school's academic rigor and required quality of writing and research. If a student's English skills are not high, reading, writing, communicating with group members, and giving presentations are difficult.

The best advisors and certified college counselors are required to abide by highly ethical and professional standards. Since they consider the broad scope of options for students, they must remain impartial and pragmatic. In order to give excellent advice in the best interest of the student, they must be able to share hope and possibility and also provide realistic outcomes or even criticism.

Third, fabricating "evidence" of research, projects, talent, academic success, and testing is not just morally wrong, it is strategically ill-advised. Some companies agree to take the test, enroll and complete classes, write the essays, complete the applications, create and finish research projects, invent technology, and reinvent transcripts from fictitious schools. Some will even pose as you in interviews. This is not only unethical for them, but students can be held responsible and disciplined by any college that finds out. At any time in the future, even decades later, a degree can be nullified if it was earned under false pretenses.

Fourth, some companies claim to have secret, special connections with Ivy League admissions officers that will ensure admissions into those schools. Many families look for the back door into admissions and there are only a few. That does not mean there are none, but the keys to those few doors are not ethically in the hands of whomever you hire. While there are candidates recruited for their fame, tied to a leader's coattails, or come from families who donate millions of dollars, the numbers of these students are small. Furthermore, universities must avoid the impression of impropriety and certainly would not allow the agent to publicize this information to other potential clients.

Are there "top secret" algorithms to the essays, tests, interviews, or admissions considerations that an agent has access to and can share with only a select few people? Of course not. Even if there were, the real magic in life, career success, and admissions is determination, discipline, diligence, intelligence, perspective, creativity, imagination, initiative, and hard work. If you owned a company, who would you hire if you had a choice? Would you hire the person who cheated or the one who was responsible, respectable, reliable, and talented?

Recent news stories have highlighted instances where agents have bought access to admissions officers from top colleges. However, the college admissions community and those who have been truthful in the admissions process are justifiably angry that this type of collusion goes on anywhere. However, some agencies have been identified and accused in public. There is also evidence supporting the fact that a host of unethical application practices have taken place. As more details are uncovered and colleges are exposed, be careful that you are not part if this growing scandal.

Fifth, some companies use a tactic called, "bait and switch." The agents or advisors whom you hire tell you that you will work with him or her. You want their expertise, but when it comes to meetings, you actually work with some low paid trainee who has far less experience. They use expensive advertising to tell you about their acclaimed leader, fancy surroundings, uniquely-tailored program, and high tech resources. You end up paying a high price, however, not for the expert wisdom from the experienced and knowledgeable leader, but for one with little experience. The switch happens after you sign the contract and you work with a different advisor rather than the one with whom you signed the contract.

Sixth, admissions officers readily declare that the best students will be discovered and no agent, advisor, or counselor is needed. Colleges search for and keep their eye out for academic and creative superstars. A top national athlete will be discovered by athletic recruiters who often send handwritten letters to show that they are definitely interested or at least have respect for the athlete's talent. President's and CEO's children are often invited to apply by private school development offices. Winners of research and innovation awards, published in a newspaper or journal article, are encouraged to apply. If you are spectacular, schools will find you directly. No agent must represent you, though sometimes they can provide advice throughout the process.

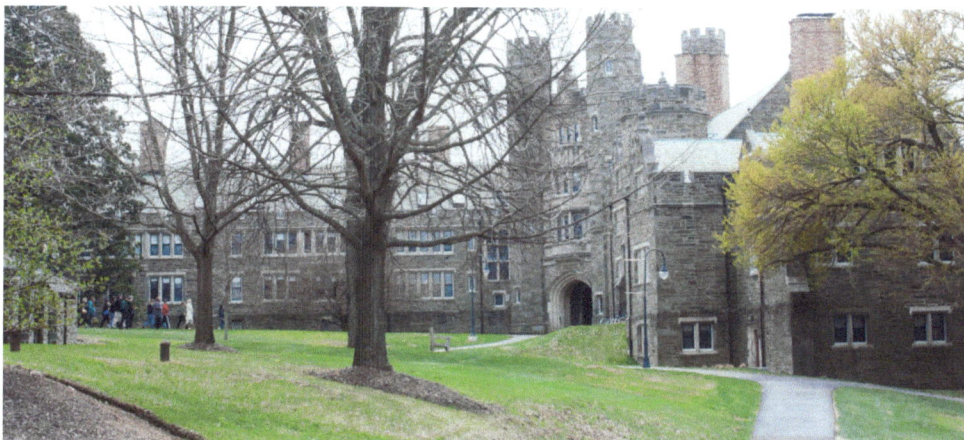

Photo Credit: Michelle C. Tahan

Chapter 4

The Good and Bad of Test Preparation/Agent Companies

The Good and Bad of Test Preparation/ Agent Companies

Importance of Preparing for Standardized Tests

Many students know they will eventually attend college, but the thought is often distantly on the horizon. The motivation for investigating colleges is often not heightened until the year before they are to apply. However, the looming and much more immediate problem is test preparation. Students are often introduced to the world of advising and agents when they begin to prepare for their standardized tests. Early test preparation is necessary.

English grammar, reading, writing, and vocabulary are a large part of the test. Some may tell you that vocabulary is not tested, but you cannot comprehend what you cannot understand. Thus, vocabulary is important throughout the test. Writing the required essay is also a significant stumbling block for many students. Practice in how to organize thinking around the prompt and writing the essay is helpful. Finally, mathematics is a strength for some, but practice in doing the problems in the way the specific standardized test presents them is valuable. First, the questions can be different than what you have seen before. Second, the topics may not be ones that you are currently learning. For example, arithmetic questions are not practiced as much in the last three years of high school. Third, standardized test questions are simply different in form than those you may have practiced in the past. Fourth, if your goal is to earn a top score, you need to practice the hard questions and those that are easy. Do not miss going over information that would be easy to review.

While it is true that some schools do not even require tests, most do. Remember, if you do not get a good score, there are still colleges that will consider you. Look up FairTest.org for a current list of colleges and universities that do not require the ACT or SAT. However, test scores are important at most of the top schools. The fact is that if you have low scores, admission at a top college or university is highly improbable. This means that you must do what top students do who go to top schools. They prepare

Start Preparing For Tests Early

Test preparation must be done early. Although less selective schools may not require ACT/SAT scores, the TOEFL/IELTS is almost always required. Some schools will not even consider a student with low scores. If you are looking to attend a top school, start practicing.

and ensure they know what is expected. You do not need to pay thousands of dollars, however, a good test preparation book is worth the cost. It is true that test preparation can sometimes be expensive for families. However, there are books that cost very little and also free supplemental materials online that do not require tutors or group classes.

Although admissions officers frequently say that test preparation is unnecessary, that is not true. The fact is a student does not intrinsically know what will be on any test. Thus, they cannot be ready. Blindly entering the testing facility, without review, is just not smart. Frankly, an admissions officer would not walk into a job interview for their next position without preparing. So, why should you fail to prepare for your admissions tests?

Students should have some prior knowledge of the general material on the test. Most students who fully embrace and dedicate themselves to test prep will often say that they learned more vocabulary, grammar, writing, and math during this intensive preparation. There are key features on the test that are important to know and strategies for testing that can improve a student's score. If nothing else, reviewing English and mathematics for the standardized tests is not a waste of time if the student learns more information that will make them more prepared and knowledgeable for college. Thus, test preparation is valuable.

Choosing A Tutor/Teacher

Some test prep teachers are very good and highly empowering. The right person can take a good student and help them become great. The student can learn how to rise to the challenge and truly believe in themselves. Confidence may seem like an insignificant component in the learning, admissions, and career advancement process, but this self-worth can empower an individual to believe they can achieve their goals. The tutor/teacher can also inspire a student to put in additional effort, become more focused, and organize their study skills approach.

If you choose to hire a tutor/teacher, find out who is leading the class and do not base your decision to hire a tutor or group based on the overall look and feel of the building. Like all individuals, humans have great variation in ability, style, personality, communication, and knowledge. While some may be touted as the best tutor/teacher available anywhere because they earned high scores when they took the test, this does not mean they are good communicators or effective teachers. Test preparation advertising often claims that all of the tutors/teachers attended top universities. The same lesson holds true; you are not hiring them because they attended a good university, but because you want to get into a good university. Remember, you want to make sure that you can learn from them. Just because they went to a top college does not automatically make them a good tutor/teacher for you.

The motivational part is critically important. Remember, it is the student who needs to study for and ultimately take the test. They must be inspired, challenged, and willing to study in order to achieve success. Even those who are not initially motivated can become determined when they believe they can succeed. With enough effort and knowledge any student can take control of their destiny.

Whether referred to in the literature as "cognitive persistence" "deliberate practice" "grit" "conscientiousness" "locus of control" or simply old-fashioned "hard work," time and again research has proven that this trait is *the key determinant of success in most task-based endeavors,* even more than aptitude, relationship skills, or simple random "luck". A good college advisor should stress this proven lesson first, foremost, and continuously in the admissions process. More importantly, any role model should believe in and live by this belief. For reasons that are still not clear, many test prep companies and agents do not focus on emphasizing the simple fact that a huge amount of focused, sustained mental effort is necessary for long-term success in a wide array of fields.

Agents Use Test Prep As A Hook to Secure Clients

Since students see the choice of a particular college as one that is off in the distance and they know a high test score is required for admission to most top schools, test preparation is the entry way to get students started walking along the college admissions road. This is often the hook that brings the students to an agent or advising company. The thought is that if they can get you to sign up for their tutoring services that you need first, they can keep you for their extended services that they offer later.

Agents know that students who go to a test preparation agency and develop a relationship with them are more likely to stay. Thus, many agents changed their way of doing business in order to get students to sign up with them first by offering SAT/ACT/TOEFL/IELTS/GAC test prep. Test preparation provides a lure to bring students into their offices.

Pedigree Does Not Determine Ability

Just because a test prep teacher went to Harvard or Cambridge, it does not mean they are good teachers!!!

This is also true for agents and advisors. You need to be able to work well with whomever you hire. You are paying lots of money and you do not want to be disappointed.

Agents and Test Prep Agencies Are Often One and the Same

Agents know that it is harder to get a student to sign up with their agency if they have gone to a test preparation agency first, particularly if that test preparation service has now decided to add college counseling services.

The reverse is also true. Some test preparation companies, who never did advising, started to offer counseling and advising. A few began offering these services even without any training or experience in counseling. They recognized that they had a pool of students seeking help in the college admissions process and started offering this service to their test prep students.

The advertising hook process, thus, starts with the importance of test preparation and how "smart" their tutors/teachers are. They explain that the help they offer will lead students to their dream schools and, thus, they can achieve the success they desire in life. If they throw in a guarantee that you will get your money back, then you have no reason not to sign up. Right?

This gimmick is convincing and it works for many people. There is nothing wrong with advertising either, but the caution here is to realize (1) they are primarily interested in the high price they will get for their agent services in the future when they get you into the door and (2) their guarantee is contingent upon a few factors that are hidden inside of their contract. This means that you must read the contract very carefully.

Deceptive Practices in Test Preparation

The goal for any student or parent is to improve test scores to the highest level possible. High scores do not equal admission to the top universities, but they are, nevertheless, required in order to be considered. Therefore, to get to the starting block and have admissions officers actually read through the entire application, high grades and scores are required.

Since "transcripts" at many Chinese high schools must be reconstructed in order to fit Western education systems, test scores on the TOEFL/IELTS and ACT/SAT are often an important factor in determining admission. There is no doubt that schools in China are often rigorous and intense, but even the best schools under the Chinese system may not prepare students for the most rigorous education in the Western system. Chinese education is different, mostly focused on memorization, while Western education tends to emphasize and encourage critical thinking skills and independent thought.

Though some measurement analysts argue that the tests do not measure aptitude or intelligence, college admissions is frequently based upon these scores. In these cases, standardized tests are intended to serve as a way for Western schools to determine quantitative/qualitative ability, critical reasoning, and knowledge acquisition for students across the globe.

This has made test preparation in China a booming business. Therefore, test prep companies focus on advertising high success rates, special curricula, and the best instructors. As a result of everyone claiming that they are the best, filling all of the spaces for students has become more competitive.

In order to ensure that the parents believe that a company is the "most qualified and successful", they provide "evidence" in the form of dramatic improvement of scores. The best way to demonstrate how much the score has improved is to offer a practice test to get a baseline score. These tests are administered in schools, large halls, or testing centers. Many schools actually invite these test prep companies to come; these firms do not charge anything and do all of the work administering the test, scoring the student's work, and providing detailed results. It sounds great. Right?

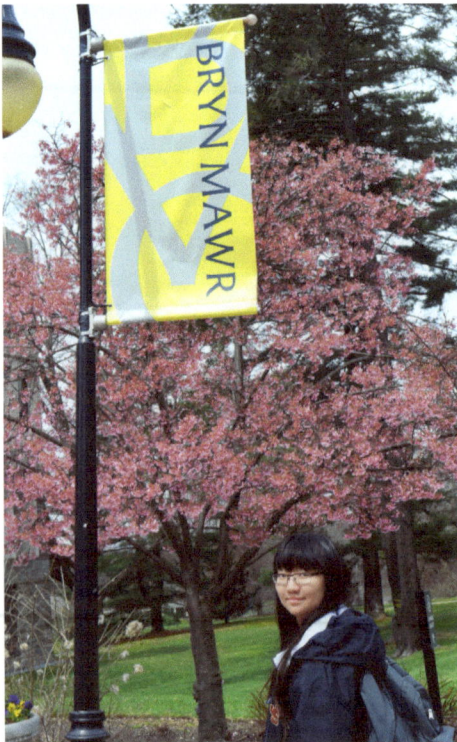

Photo Credit: Michelle C. Tahan

The initial results are often artificially low.

Test prep center administrators give a very difficult practice test in this initial testing session. The goal is to "demonstrate" that the student needs "a lot of work" in order to scare them into signing up. This first, often free, test is designed to sell the services to the student and convince the parents to pay even more because the score "is so bad".

Over the course of the test prep training, the tutor/teacher presents material and gives increasingly easier tests for each subsequent practice test session. In this way, the score continues to go up and both the parents and the students are happy. The continual progress is partly due to learning and partly due to the fact that the

Transcripts From China – Real or Fabricated?

Chinese high schools do not give grades in the way they are given in the West. In fact, most Chinese students sit in the same classroom all day with the same group of students. Thus, "transcripts" are made up of classes that are reconstructed to fit Western educational systems. Sometimes, when the Chinese school cannot recreate classes and grades, the transcript is "fabricated". The transcript often includes many more courses than a typical American high school student would take and the grades are often inflated.

Without an assurance that the grades are a true reflection of a student's learning, test scores become a key factor in determining admission. For those who do not know, success in China is based on an all-encompassing test, the GaoKao, which qualifies students for admission to their universities.

test is easier. However, even if learning does not occur, there is a good chance the student will still get a higher score with the easier test.

The last TOEFL, IELTS, SAT, or ACT test they give as they end their training is the easiest. The score improves significantly, "proving" that the test prep agency did a good job. They report to the parents how amazing the student did when they declare that the student scored a 100+ point improvement on the SAT or 5 to 8 point improvement on the ACT or TOEFL.

This is how they can give a "money back guarantee". They just need to show that, after their lessons, the student has now earned a significantly higher score, with statistics to prove this. The fact is that the student would have actually received a higher score either way from the beginning with the easier test. Given that the student has become more comfortable with testing conditions, is more able to focus on similar problems, and surely must have learned something in the hundreds of hours of exposure to the material, the company does not have to worry. Whatever amount of learning may have happened in between, it does not matter because the final test will show that the student's test score improved, by at least the amount guaranteed, with a 99% probability. Thus, it is easy to make that guarantee.

The true problem becomes evident when the student takes the actual test. At that point, if the student does poorly, there is typically a clause that says that actual scores for the official proctored test may vary due to test anxiety. When the student takes the "real" test, the scores are often significantly lower and the test prep company is not liable to give the money back. This is a very popular and commonly used tactic in the test prep industry. While some companies genuinely offer valuable test preparation services, it would be incredibly difficult to prove that a test prep maker intentionally created an ineffective system due to financial interests and low tutor/teacher productivity. Many test prep makers use "proprietary" or unofficial practice tests because they claim they do not want to break copyright laws from using the actual TOEFL, IELTS, SAT, and ACT tests. However, these tests sometimes do not mirror the actual tests.

The best way around this is to thoroughly prepare on your own or hire reputable companies.

The sites below all offer either free or reasonably priced options to take real practice questions from the TOEFL, SAT, and ACT, respectively.

https://www.ets.org/toefl/ibt/prepare

https://collegereadiness.collegeboard.org/sat/practice/full-length-practice-tests

http://www.act.org/content/act/en/products-and-services/the-act/test-preparation/act-online-prep.html

Any responsible test preparation advisor will tell you that a determined candidate who puts in hundreds of hours of focused practice can get very similar results as a student who takes even the best test prep courses. While this book may stress skepticism about promises made in the educational advising business, there are very good test prep companies. You just need to do the research and be willing to do the work, remembering that effort and commitment are more important than a center's tutors or teachers. Get help if you believe that the lessons will be valuable. Study on your own if you have the discipline to do so.

Photo Credit: Michelle C. Tahan

Chapter 5

Advocate for Yourself - No
Special Permissions Needed

Advocate for Yourself - No Special Permissions Needed

I t is perfectly okay not to be an Olympic athlete, a master musician, an ultra-wealthy scion, or a Nobel Laureate. Many students get into top colleges and universities that are not even close. However, it is unethical for any college advisor to guarantee that he or she can get you "special treatment" for a huge fee.

Even though Asian societies typically have a direct instruction model, where instructors provide knowledge and the students follow his or her lead, the West expects a greater level of inquisitiveness, critical thinking, and problem solving ability. The focus in the West is less on memorization and more on thinking through a set of scenarios. Figuring out how a process works is more important than knowing the names or parts.

From an academic, professional, and social standpoint, the admissions process requires thinking through a multistep process, particularly for international students. International students must take tests and apply like other students, but there is an additional TOEFL/IELTS test. After submission of the application, there are bank statements and visa/passport/proof of residency documents. Following through is not a simple task. However, this process always begins with presenting an application directly to admissions in an authentic way.

While varsity sports, clubs, honors, and activities are not stressed in China the same way as in the West, and there is less access to opportunities for research projects, leadership, or internships, this should not stop you from applying. Additionally, it is not necessary to fabricate activities in order to fit into the Western style of education. American colleges and universities who work with Chinese students know that these opportunities to get involved are simply not the same. Merely showing inquisitive thinking and taking meaningful action that produces real- world results is often the best way to demonstrate your passion, action, and commitment.

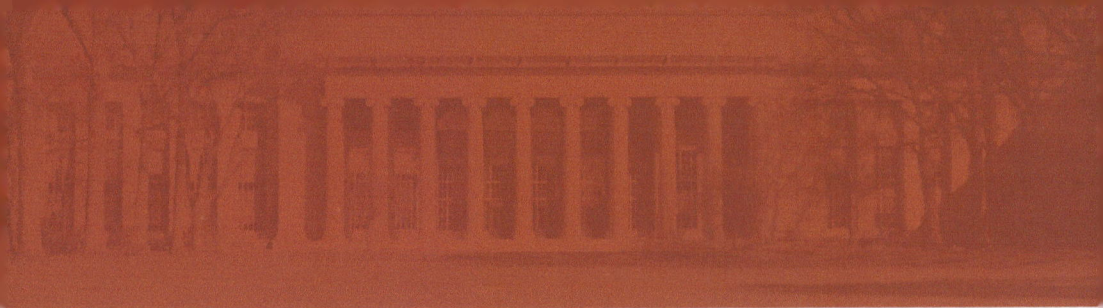

Learn to Ask for What You Want

The West prides itself on having students advocate for themselves, set up meetings/interviews on their own, and take initiative.

Interview

If you speak English well, see if you can interview online through their virtual service like Skype, Google Hangouts, GoToMeeting, Adobe Connect, or other video conferencing software the university uses. Interviews are a great way to present yourself.

You can contact schools or check the university's website to see whether or not they offer interviews in person or virtually. Some do, some do not. It is possible that you can meet with a representative on their college campus or when they come into your area for a college admissions trip. There are also alumni who interview students and send an evaluation back to the home campus to be included in the application file. Other times, the interview is just informational so that you can learn more about the school. Finally, there are outside organizations that interview students on behalf of the university. Sometimes these are recorded and the recording is sent to the school and sometimes a written evaluation is submitted.

Whatever the interview scenario, the key is to demonstrate authentic interest in the unique mix of learning opportunities that each university presents in its own way. If you can articulate why a particular educational program at a particular school is an excellent match for your individual personality, you have more substance than about 95% of candidates who never took enough time to deeply research and consider such an answer so thoroughly.

Above all else, the West prides itself on being an "open society". No introductions, special permissions, etc. are needed. This means that you should not have to pay someone to be considered. This also means that you should take the initiative to ask for what you want and create the future you desire. While you must follow the rules, if you can articulate what you want and make good arguments for why you should be interviewed, accepted, or hired, you are halfway there.

Do Your Own Research

You can gain acceptance to college if you present yourself authentically. Even if you have an advisor, you should look into colleges on your own. Research can aid you in making decisions about where you want to attend. While an advisor may assist you, ultimately you will attend and you should take action in order to make sure you are headed for a school you will like.

One of the authors' students came from a remote part of China for high school and "ended up" at a small school in Pittsburgh where his host family did not have heat in the house and he was put in the basement where he slept and studied. While you are considering colleges, it would be wise to take the appropriate steps to ensure that you will not find yourself in the same situation. The point is that you might wind up attending a school where the area is dangerous, the students are not friendly, the teachers are more focused on their research, or it simply is not the best fit for you. There will be challenges no matter where you go, but you can avoid a bad situation by doing thorough research. You will be glad you did. Just because someone tells you that they liked it does not mean you will. Plus, the point of this book is that agents are paid by the school to convince you to attend. They do not get paid unless you go, so they may tell you it is great either way because it is in their best interest, not yours.

Long Term Planning

Long-term planning works. You do not have to wait to consider colleges until your junior year. You will miss opportunities if you do. Besides, you will discover what colleges offer and your research could lead to a much better experience. The real opportunity lies in growing as a person and as a scholar. You might find and attend a summer program where you learn more about your potential major, like engineering, business, medicine, environmental science, law, or journalism. You may choose to take a college class at a college or university you are considering. More importantly, long-term success stems from being prepared and knowing what is ahead.

An advisor can help you with this research and possibly provide you a tool to organize the information you collect, however, only your persistence will lead to your success.

Why Universities Hire Agents

There are many reasons why universities hire agents. The majority of these are not nefarious, though from the outside looking in, it may seem like the university is paying off agents on the one hand and, at the same time, chastising them for inappropriate actions on the other. Many colleges and universities are looking outside of their country to attract qualified, talented, and motivated students. Some of these students may not have heard about their school.

It's Your Life -
Do the Research

Since this is your future, you want to make sure you find a place where you can live, learn, and thrive.

You want to do your own in-depth research because, ultimately, you might find yourself in a place where you have few choices and must abide by very different rules than you expected.

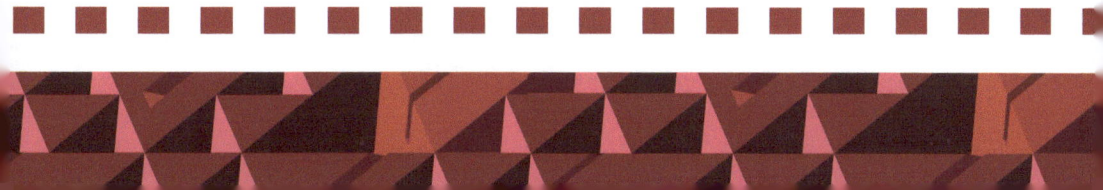

Below is a short list of reasons why universities may want to hire agents from a survey we conducted. More research is necessary, but our intent is to continue to gather data on agents, universities, and their relationships.

1. Universities hire agents to promote their school.

2. They seek to find the best students.

3. College seek a diverse student body.

4. Some universities do not have experience in Asia. They want to hire individuals who have extensive knowledge of this market.

5. The university needs to bring in additional money from out-of-state/international student tuition.

6. It is easier for them to reach their recruitment goals with the work of agents.

7. They do not want to be held accountable for the talent and academic ability of the students they accept. In this way, they can blame the agents for students who are unprepared.

8. When colleges do not require Chinese students to submit test scores for admission, they do not have to count them in the admissions statistics for ranking purposes.

Constant and Persistent Learning is Required

Some people, the authors of this book included, were not aware of what was happening in Asia before we spent considerable time traveling to various cities and countries across the Pacific. This narrow mindedness is reduced with every experience. While we are well traveled, we cannot claim to know everything about all regions and all types of students.

For example, most people are amazed to learn that hundreds of English speaking bachelor's programs in Europe are tuition free or offered at a very low cost to foreigners. Some programs in the United Kingdom, Ireland, South Africa, New Zealand, Australia, and Canada are actually more rigorous than famous universities in the United States. While studying in the United States may be attractive, the travel and immigration benefits of these other universities may be equally enticing. Particularly with the uncertainty from the recent U.S. election, students need to consider possible implications. Currency exchange rates have also been mentioned by students and families as a concern.

Experience Counts

Even experienced counselors need to continue to learn and as they do, they become wise about the college admissions landscape.

You too must commit yourself to constant and persistent learning in order to stay current in your field. Any career you choose will change dramatically over the next 20 years and, with technology interventions, may actually be unrecognizable.

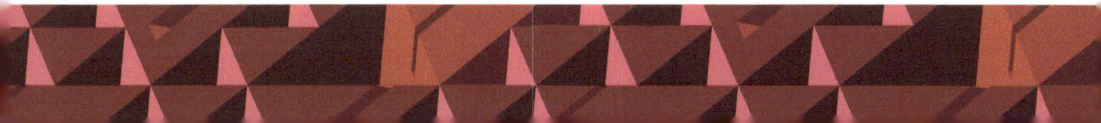

Another point is important to note. An admissions consultant who charges $1,000 USD an hour generously donated her time to give a free school presentation at a Chinese school. During the presentation, she even admitted she was not familiar with the comprehensive merits of many California community colleges. The consultant was clearly knowledgeable about her specific area, but knowing the benefits at a wide range of schools requires constant learning.

If talented advisors within a country lack the knowledge common to others, this demonstrates that the territory of college admissions is very dynamic, complex and extensive. Few people truly have a thorough and global understanding of the merits of all major university systems in the United States, much less the world. This does not discount the wisdom of many experienced consultants, but it does emphasize the fact that there is so much to know.

Very good college counselors travel and visit dozens of colleges each year to keep up to date with the territory, visit new schools, meet with students, and talk to the current admissions representatives that change more frequently than you might think. The best advisor for you is one who can give you the information you need on a broad enough scale to help you reach your goals.

Thinking Outside of the Box

Perhaps the most effective function of an advisor can be in helping you narrow down your choices so that you can focus on your research. There are over 50,000 properly accredited higher education institutions in the world, each having their individual merits. Most of their doors are open to international students and many of the tuition and living costs are very reasonable. Some are even free.

Since we live in an interconnected world, it is helpful to think globally. There are many merits of systems outside the United States. While you may still choose to attend college within the United States, it is good to explore your options. You might be surprised at what you will find. There are also study abroad programs within most colleges that will allow you to gain a global perspective during your four years of school. Internships at companies where you can gain experience are valuable too. During your four years of college, make sure you prepare for your career while you are still in school. Investigate the internships and study abroad programs your university offers.

No matter what major you choose, you will discover other areas that interest you. You may decide to dual major or minor in another focus area, as well as discover areas in which you are curious. Talk to dorm mates, classmates, and professors about topics you find fascinating. Look at the best-reviewed professors at www.ratemyprofessors. com/blog/toplist. Often, you can even view their acclaimed course websites or contact them to see if you can capture what makes their teaching wonderful.

Search Google or other web resources for experts in your fields of interest and email people until you find answers. Throughout this process, you might have the chance to communicate with Nobel Laureates, distinguished scientists, economists, and philanthropists. You just need to be genuinely curious. You might even discover that a previously unheard of field is the right one for you. With over a thousand academic concentrations and majors, as well as opportunities for independent study and even self-designed concentrations, there is surely something out there that can capture your genuine interest.

With over 7,000 higher education institutions in the United States alone, there is no limit to opportunities to meet professors who might be able to open academic or social doors for you. Write notes to people, ask for advice, and gather more information along the way. Professors love to hear that their research has been read beyond the typical people who peruse academic journals. They are eager to find that their work touched the imagination of people in other countries. Go out and ask questions, as it can lead to research and career opportunities. Your quest might truly be life changing.

Photo Credit: Michelle C. Tahan

Chapter 6

Universities Want to Work Directly With Students; They Hate Agents

Universities Want to Work Directly With Students; They Hate Agents

High schools in China are filled with students whose dreams vary, but most want a better life, greater opportunities, and the chance to fulfill their family's vision of success. Sometimes this means studying abroad. This was clearly evident at a Beijing high school where speaking to the entire school meant having a few hundred eager students ask questions about their future, colleges abroad, and how to gain admission. Experiences talking to students in Shanghai, Hong Kong, Guangzhou, Shenzhen, Guiyang, Urumqi, and Hohhot, were similar. While students apply to schools around the world, the United Kingdom and the United States were the most popular destinations with Australia not far behind according to data from the Chinese Ministry of Education.

Serving as a college admissions counselor for Beijing Public High School 80, Joe Klunder booked over one hundred universities to give presentations, either online or in-person. His initiative made his school a destination stop for colleges. Many of the colleges were eager to accept Joe's offer to speak at his school or present their school online, in part because they prefer meeting and communicating with students personally. When they can visit schools in person, they appreciate the offer.

On the UCLA website, the university specifically issued a cautionary statement, "Important Message About Agents and Consultants," that UCLA does not work with agents and agents do not represent the university in the admissions process. Furthermore, the use of agents "is not endorsed by UCLA." They go on to discuss the ethical reasons, violations, and decision to revoke an admission offer, cancel admission, and withdraw students who violate their principles in admission.

Direct Access to Students

Colleges prefer to have direct access to high schools and their students, though this is not always easy. A high school speaking opportunity for a college is a way to connect with students rather than going through a third party.

From the UCLA website:

"UCLA Undergraduate Admission does not partner with agents to represent the University or to administer any part of the application process. The engagement of agents or private organizations for the purpose of recruiting or enrolling international students is not endorsed by UCLA.

UCLA expects an application to be the work of the student and any deviation violates University policy which may lead to rejection of application materials, revocation of an admission offer, cancellation of admission, or involuntary withdrawal from the University. There is no formula for gaining admission to UCLA. Students with vastly different credentials come from thousands of secondary schools across the country and around the world. What unifies our students are the talents they bring to UCLA and their passion to explore all that UCLA has to offer."

https://www.admission.ucla.edu/prospect/intl.htm#transfer

University representatives want to work directly with students if at all possible. There are many complications related to working with agents, including the ethics of monetizing the admissions process. In this way, they can get to know the student better without the intervention of an outside party, describe the opportunities at their school, and invite them to connect personally with their students, faculty, research, and programs.

Admissions officers are often willing to make the time to connect online, even when it may seem unreasonable in the middle of the night in another time zone. Most people in admissions are well aware that the recruitment process is not a 9am to 5pm job. This work often requires meeting when it is convenient to the student. Fortunately for e-mail, the ability to asynchronously communicate is a benefit. However, do not discount communicating synchronously too.

Photo Credit: Michelle C. Tahan

Most individuals in admissions would rather talk to you at midnight in person rather than work with an agent. If the agent tells you differently, they are not telling the truth. Though there might be a few admissions officers who feel differently, universities want to talk directly with you, even if it is inconvenient for them. Some will even conduct Skype presentations to students well beyond their "normal" working hours.

Some colleges and universities want to attract more students to apply. However, even extremely popular schools like Columbia University or Oxford University are willing to go beyond the call of duty to help students throughout the world. They, too, want students who are a good fit and will add to their community of scholars. It is also in their best interests. Do not hesitate to contact universities directly. They may not respond, depending upon the demands of their schedule, but do not be surprised if they do. It is well worth the effort.

In one instance, Ms. Charlotte Isaacs, an Oxford University admissions representative, was welcomed at Beijing Public High School 80 in person to an eager group of students. Sophisticated and patient, she answered everyone's questions and took the time to tour the campus.

Ms. Isaacs explicitly said, "I do not work with agents. Oxford University does not like agents and will stay away from applicants who use them to package their applications." Although she represents one of the most selective undergraduate institutions in the world, many university admissions officers will say the same thing in the same tone. *If an admissions officer knows that a student worked with an agent, or suspects that an essay has been changed, copied, or embellished, they are likely to completely disregard the application.*

The other important point, though, is that this visit would not have happened without an early direct communication with her and a straightforward inquiry. You are encouraged to contact university admissions representatives. They are looking for you too.

Disastrous Results Have Caused Alarm

Some universities that work with agents get disastrous results. Some students come to the United States with very little English and cannot read or write on a high enough level. Though English proficiency programs are often offered in association with many universities, the required level of English often necessitates multiple non-credit English classes to get up to speed. Failing to understand, while listening to English, spoken fast, is a serious problem. While some students carry a translator, this only works well if the student can keep up with the translation. Outside of class reading is frequently cumbersome with long and difficult assignments that are nearly impossible to complete even for those who are fluent in English. Furthermore, if students cannot communicate with classmates, they have trouble with group assignments and are sometimes not included in conversations.

Agents Are Not Highly Regarded

If an admissions officer knows that a student worked with an agent, or suspects that tests/ transcripts are fabricated, or an essay has been changed, copied, or highly embellished, they are likely to completely disregard the application.

The entire process of going to college in another city is daunting, but in another country, it is even tougher. There is a sense of culture shock that many freshmen face. With new rules, living conditions, and study requirements, this shock is intensified when students must also negotiate different education systems and ways of learning. Students, who are sometimes not emotionally mature, must jump over academic, language, financial, and social hurdles.

For students whose English is not as strong as their TOEFL score presents, questions arise. Furthermore, the Chinese student begins to feel like an imposter. Sometimes the Chinese student wonders whether or not they deserve to attend the university and whether or not the experience is worth the enormous effort, particularly when they entered the college unethically. Some used fake credentials or essays they did not write. Feeling cast aside because of the lack of speaking or listening skills in group projects, they sometimes isolated themselves. When alone, some turn to alcohol, drugs, video games, or simply go shopping rather than focus on their studies. This, however, only lowers their grades more until they fail a class, are put on academic probation, or kicked out of school entirely.

Although parents paid for their children to receive a college education, the students cannot often get the good grades their parents expect. Sometimes this means that they copy off other people's papers, find someone to write their papers, or get another person to take their tests. Occasionally, this leads to being caught for plagiarism or academic integrity violations. The process of being accused, defending his or her actions, and other students finding out leads to more problems. Sometimes they are even kicked out of school and told to return home.

In the May 2015 *Newsweek* article, "U.S. Colleges Expelled As Many As 8,000 Chinese Students In 3 Years," this point is clearly made. Additionally, the article explains that the students may have been recruited because they would bring money into the school, since they would not be offered financial aid, yet were not properly supported in being successful when they arrived. Additionally, the U.S. Department of Justice indicted some students for using the college admissions system in the United States for the sole purpose of obtaining visas.

This embarrassment and shame, particularly within a family that sacrificed their savings for the hope that their child would come back and be able to provide for his or her parents, leads some students to commit suicide in college. All-in-all, this has become a huge problem for colleges. Since college admissions officers care about

Steep Learning Curve

Since the learning curve to assimilate into American Universities is high, the students must make a choice to adapt to the culture or simply maintain their home culture and primarily make friends with other Chinese students. In this way, they can speak Chinese and not have to develop the colloquial knowledge of the American language and culture.

students and want them to thrive, they do not want to put them in a situation where they will fail. It is not fair to the student. It is not fair to the parents. It is not fair to the colleges. The agent was paid either way.

Chinese Flock Together

Though this is not always the case, many Chinese students prefer to attend colleges with other Chinese students. In this way, they have a network of students with whom to communicate, share a common language, and get involved in activities. Together, they can work on homework and go for meals at places where foods are more familiar. Although this also means that they may not be practicing English much of the time, they can feel that they belong.

Adapting to the American educational system has a high learning curve. The cultural barrier is significant. If students arrive on campus in August, just before school begins, they have little time to get used to the surroundings and culture. They must make a choice as to whether or not they will gain the social, political, and attitudinal knowledge needed to assimilate. Of course, this happens for American students attending U.S. colleges too, but the problem is compounded for the Chinese student.

Except for very independent students who want the challenge of speaking English every day to people they meet, many find students like themselves. Often, classes in the United States have group projects, trips, or activities where they work together. Collaborative activities are common in American universities. Unless a student is outgoing enough to actively participate in these types of groups, they often find it helpful to team up with other Chinese students. The goal of many faculty is to get students to meet other classmates, so expect that to occur when you attend college.

Agents, Fit, and Ethics

When considering colleges, along with the opportunity to travel abroad, the triumph and challenges of independence, and the goal of a great education, there are many factors and some pitfalls. Fitting in academically, socially, and in many other ways is important. The problem is that agents, in their quest to earn money in the booming business of getting students into school, may not be concerned about the student. There are consequences to traveling across the ocean just because you are accepted to a college. Adjusting to the environment and culture presents a whole new set of challenges.

Just as a reminder, consider how agents work. Agents get money from the university for each student who decides to attend that school. Let's say the agreement is that the agent will receive 15% of the first year's tuition, which, let's say is $30,000. So, the agent gets $4,500. The agent, then, recruits students and parents who pay for their help with applications, essays, and admissions. In this way, they get money from the college and they get money from the families. The agent convinces the student to come to a particular school where they are paid the $4,500 commission rather than choose one where the student might be a better fit. If this is extrapolated to 100 students in a year, the agent will receive $450,000 just from universities, not counting the funds they receive from the parents, which is sometimes more than what they get from the universities. So, now let's say that is $1,000,000.

Thus, the agent may not be helping the student get into the best school for them, but rather to attend a college where the agent is getting the greatest kickback. To add to that, the agent is sometimes guaranteed admission for candidates the agent brings them. He or she makes a lot of money in the process and publically takes credit for extraordinary results. There is a reason to be careful of agents, since agents will often put their own self-interest first and have little incentive to practice differently.

Photo Credit: Michelle C. Tahan

Chapter 7

Codes of Conduct for Competent Professionals

Codes of Conduct for Competent Professionals

Despite horror stories of agents not living up to their promises, there are many college advising services that are valuable and can help students understand the college admissions process. Just make sure to know how they work and hold the companies accountable for what they promise.

Professional and Ethical Counselors

There are good people in the field. The best ones may simply be teachers and college counselors at your local school. Some put your interests first and have no financial incentives for doing otherwise. Public school teachers around the world have a special code of ethics to help students, regardless of their financial background or status. There are many benefits to gaining advice from teachers and counselors; supporting students is their mission.

Second, if students plan to use outside, supplemental services such as college admissions consultants, tutors, test preparation services, etc. be clear about the rules, responsibilities, and expected outcomes. If there is a contract, read what you are signing. It may only seem like a matter of titles and words; but, examine carefully, there is a big difference between someone who has your best interests at heart and a company who simply wants to take your money and take advantage of your ignorance.

A Few Simple Rules:

Rule #1 - There Are Ethical Codes of Conduct

Unlike an uncertified agent, a professional consultant has very strict rules of practice, similar to a doctor or lawyer.

College admissions consultants give advice and assist in the process; but, do not write essays or conduct practices that are unethical under association rules.

Well-known associations for college admissions consultants include: Independent Educational Consultants Association (IECA), Higher Educational Consulting Association (HECA), National Association of College Admissions Counseling (NACAC) and the corresponding overseas branch, International Association of College Admissions Counseling (IACAC or OACAC). Each of these organizations requires an application for membership, continuing education, and a code of conduct that must be followed. Here is an example of the IECA code of conduct:

http://www.iecaonline.com/PDF/IECA_Principles_of_Good_Practice.pdf

If you want to search for the name of an individual IECA member, you can find them in the IECA directory at:

httpc;//www.iocaonlino.oom/ofm_PublioSoaroh/pg_PublioSoaroh.ofm?modo−ontry

Rule #2 - Be Wary of Promises or Guarantees of Results

Teachers can also guarantee that all students will get "A's" if they only take top students, refuse average students, drop students who have difficulties, and make the class so easy everyone earns an A. Does that make a good teacher? Of course not.

Likewise, an agent or college counselor can easily guarantee "95% of clients get into one of the top 100 universities" if they take only the top students, void the contract if they do not make a deadline, and drop any student who does not follow a certain rule. This is truly all a matter of statistics. This would mean the agent or college counselor only works with students who are so good they either do not really need extra help or they do not get candidates into a top 100 university, but simply into an English Foundation class or non-degree program affiliated with a top 100 school.

An agent can offer money-back guarantees, but will not always honor those guarantees. Read the fine print carefully. Guarantees are often a sign of deceptiveness. An old adage states, "If something seems to good to be true, it probably is." Be careful.

A college counseling professional may offer a free consultation. Many offer a competitive hourly rate, provide excellent service, and deliver testimonials. However, those who have a well-known, well-respected office with lots of clients are typically

Rules to Live By

Rule #1 - There Are Ethical Codes of Conduct

Rule #2 - Be Wary of Promises or Guarantees of Results

Rule #3 - When in Doubt, Ask for References

Rule #4 - Know the Rules of Fair Testing

booked for over a year in advance. Almost all are full in the fall during the admissions cycle. Advertising is a sign that they need clients, which they may if they are expanding. However, most students and parents find counselors based upon word of mouth and reputation. If you see advertisements on billboards, magazines, and television, make sure you ask around. Possibly they are very good, but it is also possible that they are more focused on the business aspects of the presentation to parents rather than the actual work of spending time with the student and advising. This may be a telltale sign they care more about sales, rather than service.

A good college counseling professional takes students of all abilities and assists them in reaching their educational goals by helping they find best-fit school(s). Average students most likely cannot be accepted into top ten schools, but they can get accepted into colleges corresponding to their level of ability and experience. A good college counselor will inspire students who have not lived up to their full potential and create a plan to attend a college that might serve as a stepping stone until they can prove themselves in college level coursework.

Rule #3 - When in Doubt, Ask for References

You can ask the agent if you can speak to a few of their former clients who can tell you more about the service they provide. During the conversation, you might ask them about the experience working with them and how they are different from the thousands of other self-proclaimed admissions professionals.

You might even go online to see if former clients posted reviews. Read through their website and learn more. Check out some of the other agents in order to make some comparisons. This is a big investment of time and money, learn more before you decide.

Rule #4 - Know the Rules of Fair Testing

The College Board, the company that offers the SAT I and II, the American College Test (ACT), and every accredited university have representatives who can speak to you about their rules of fair and ethical testing. At the very least, each organization provides general policy guidelines, admissions statistics, the rules of fair play, as well as consequences for not following the rules.

For example, you must have a picture identification. You may not have access to the actual questions before the test. Nobody can take the test for you. The College Board and ACT allow certain calculators and programs during the test.

These and other rules are important to know to at least prevent trouble, like disqualification.

Photo Credit: Michelle C. Tahan

Chapter 8

Final Notes

Final Notes

1. Most colleges have worked hard to build a culture of excellence with high standards of integrity. Be aware that the United States also has for-profit universities in which their reputation is very poor and getting a degree from those schools is not worth much unless you already have the job you want.

2. The number of agents in the world is hard to track because much of this work is done secretly under the radar. Any figures you find are not reliable. The numbers are manipulated as are the number of the employees and their customers. There is a genuine lack of integrity and many inflate their results.

3. Education is a solution to many problems, but students have to have the ability, motivation, persistence, and willingness to sacrifice in order to do the work. There are no real shortcuts to success. Paying someone to do the work is an option, but it is unethical and immoral. Can you imagine being flown in a plane by a pilot or being operated on by a surgeon who may have cheated, and *not* learned their craft? Why sell yourself and the others around you short by constantly trying to cheat the system, when the more direct answer is definitely more fruitful and may even be less troublesome in the end?

Photo Credit: Michelle C. Tahan

Further Reading

What follows is a suggested reading booklist. Joe Klunder has had correspondence with each of these authors over the years. Each of them possesses advanced training and degrees, has several decades of experience, and could be described as absolutely excellent in every way. Any work they have done, not only encouraged Joe to integrate their work into his, but also is his superior.

If you have found this book informative, fantastic. If you have additional comments, suggestions, and ideas about how we can enhance it, or if you have come across specific tips for dealing with agents, please let us know. This piece is a work in progress and we will continue to update it with more current information as it becomes available.

A is for Admission by Michelle Hernandez
College Finder by Steven Antonoff
Destination College by Rachel A. Winston
Fiske Guide to Colleges by Edward B. Fiske
Getting in by Standing Out by Deborah Bedor
Rock Hard Apps by Katherine Cohen

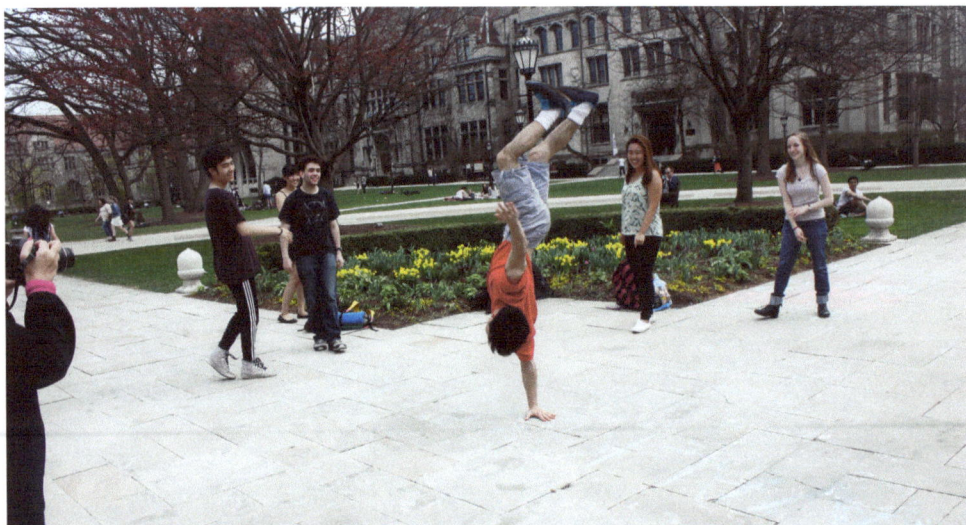

Photo Credit: Michelle C. Tahan

www.ingramcontent.com/pod-product-compliance
Lightning Source LLC
Chambersburg PA
CBHW042125080426
42734CB00001B/6